Large Print Dot-to-Dot Sea Life Puzzles From 133 to 433 Dots Dot-to-Dot Books For Adults

By Laura's Dot to Dot Therapy

How To Use This Book

Hi! We're so glad you're a lover of puzzles and dot connecting- we are too!

Connecting the dots in this book is simple- just relax and follow the numbers in consecutive order, drawing a straight line between each one. Dot 1 will connect to dot 2 and so on and so forth until there are no more dots to connect. There's always another dot and you'll always find it. Connect every dot to discover the beautiful images they create.

In case you get lost or can't find a dot, never stress- there's an answer key at the back of the book that will show you exactly where each dot connects to the next. If you want to color your images, we encourage you to do so! Feel free to try all different colors and coloring mediums for your images!

If you find any errors or omissions in this book, just email us at Laurasdottodot@gmail.com, let us know, and we will send you a free book to make up for it! We want you to have the best dot to dot experience!

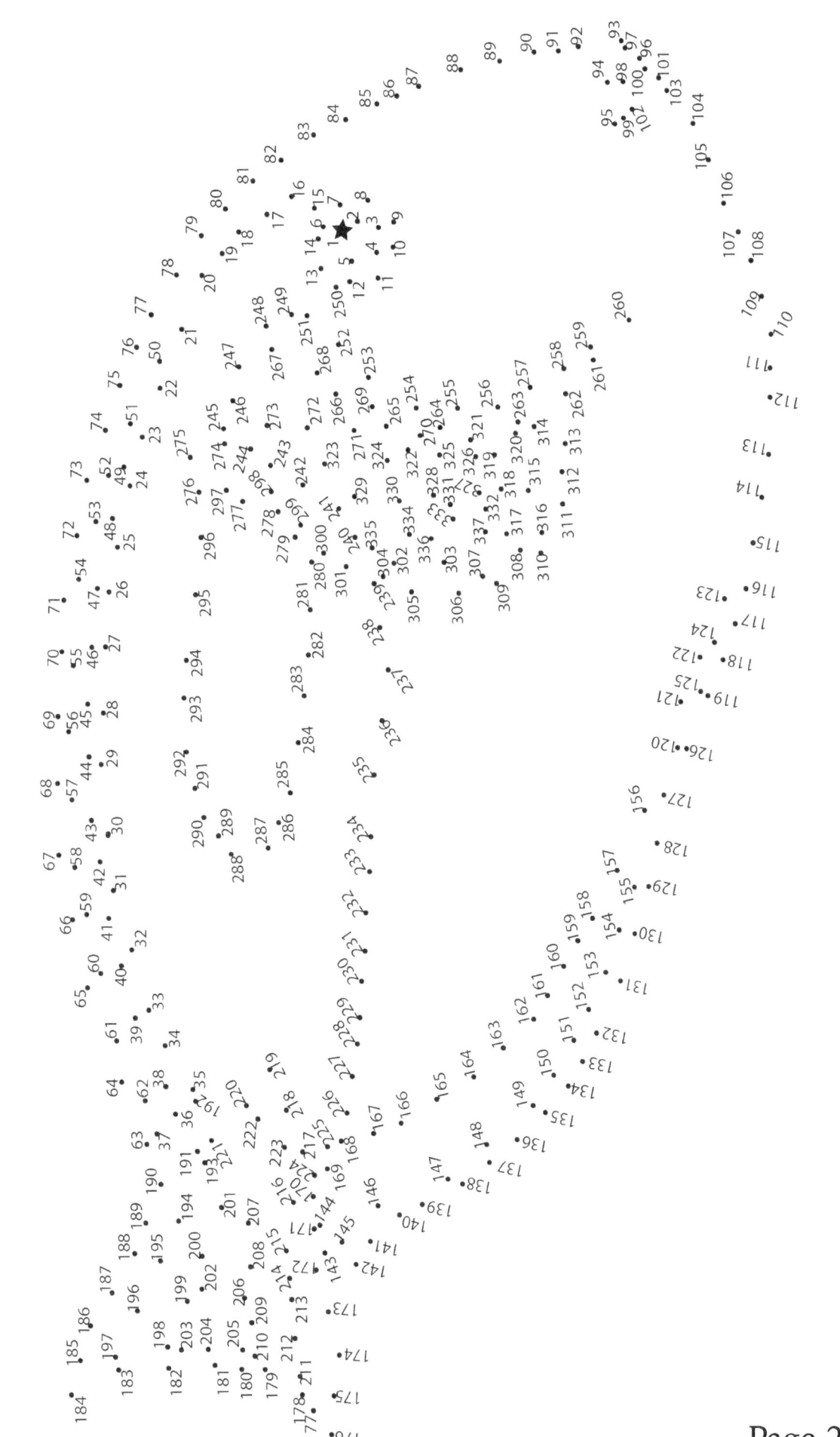

Enjoy bonus images from
some of our other fun
dot-to-dot books

Find all of our books on Amazon

Relaxing Romance By the Ocean
Dot-to-Dot For Adults

Beautiful Flowers and Butterflies
Dot-to-Dot for Adults

ANSWER KEY

Follow along with the
page numbers from top left
to bottom right

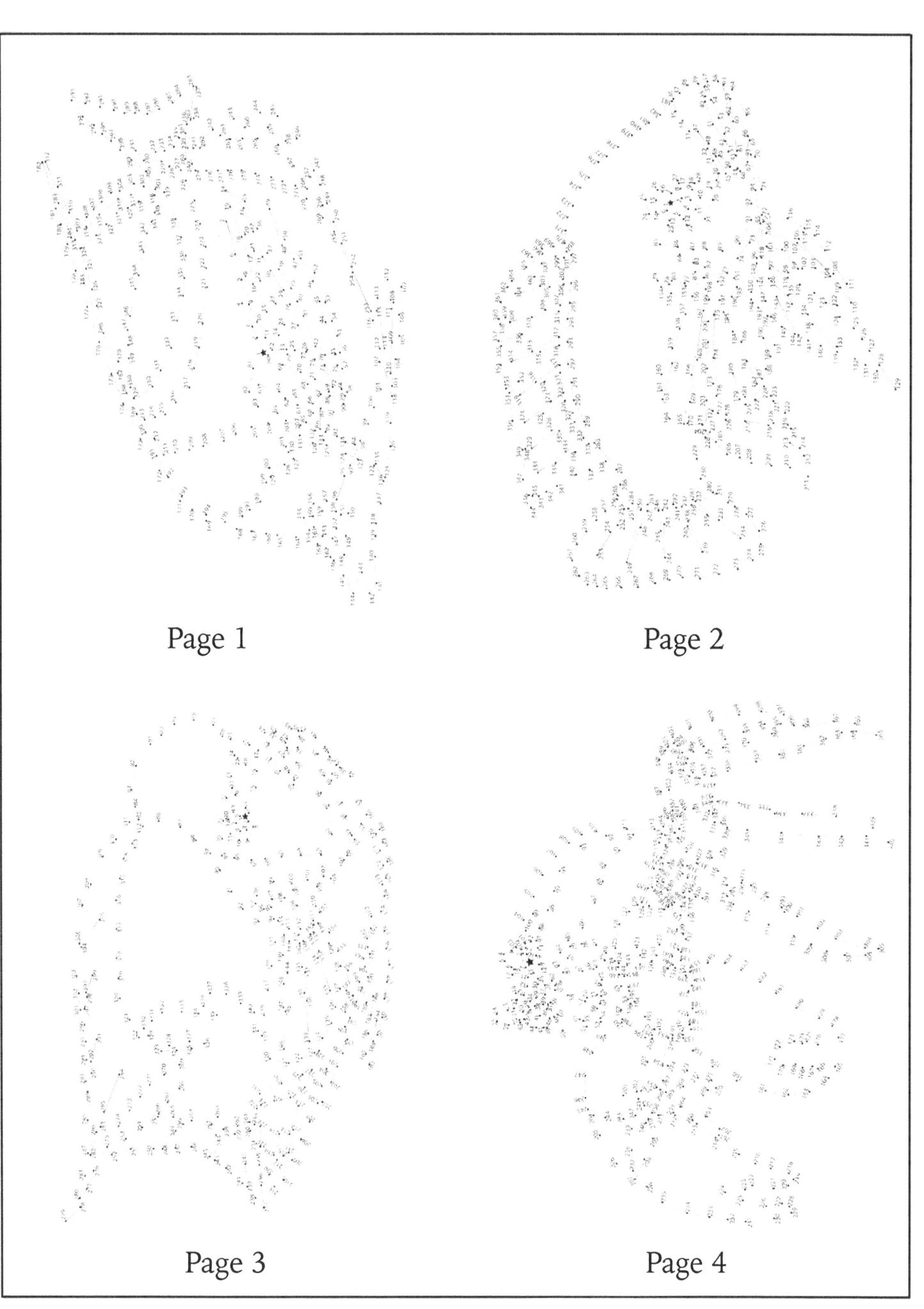

Page 1

Page 2

Page 3

Page 4

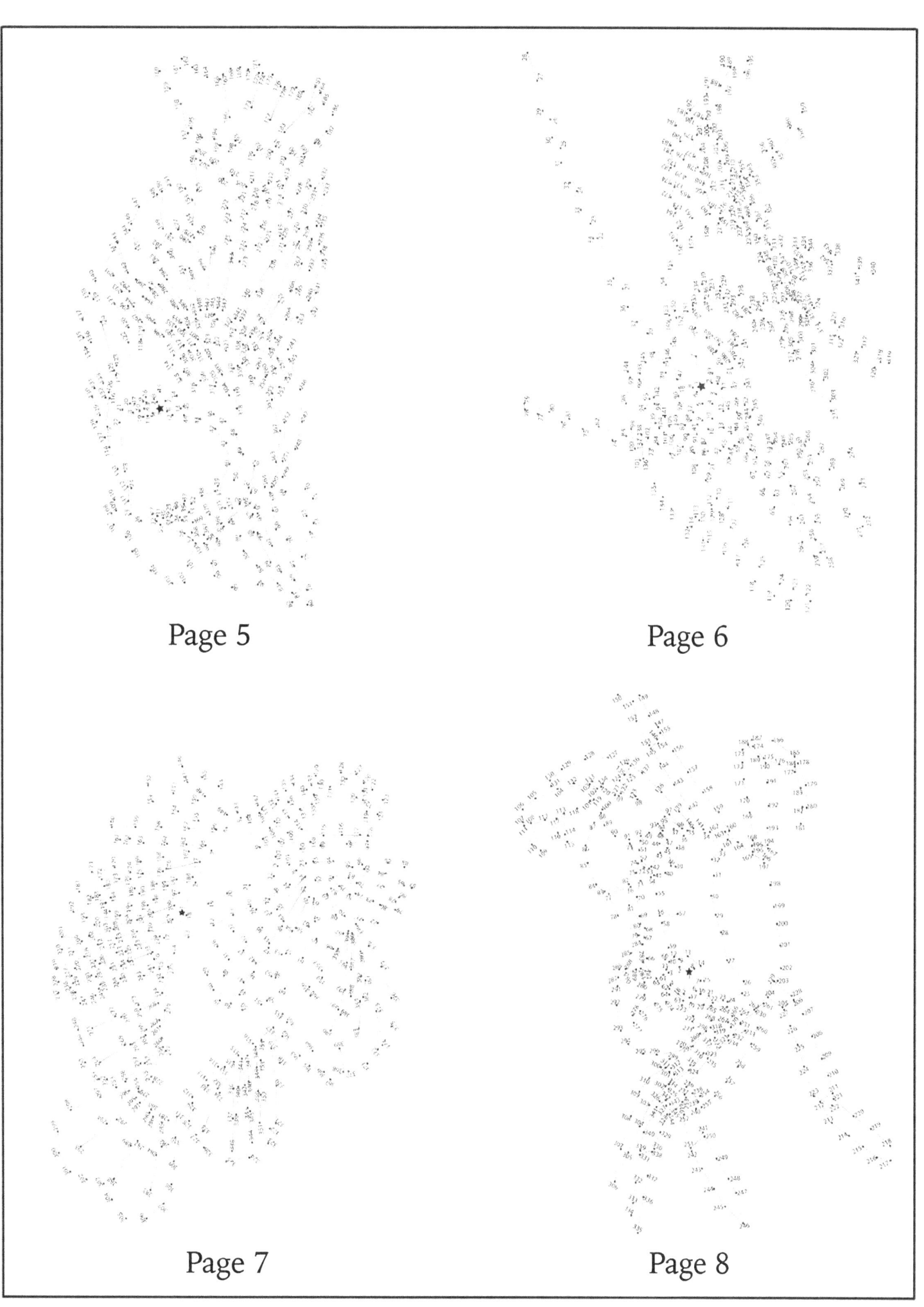

Page 5

Page 6

Page 7

Page 8

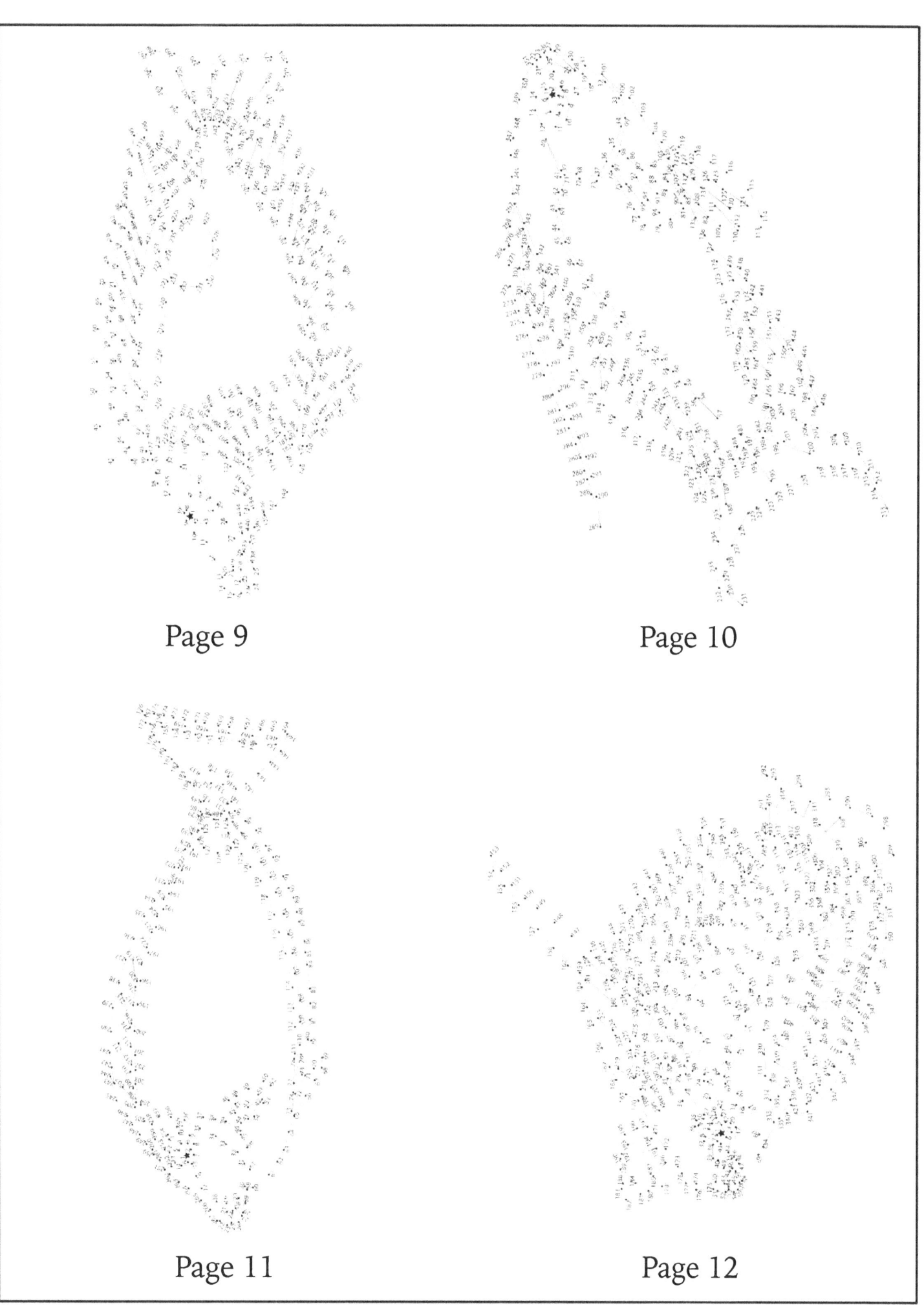

Page 9

Page 10

Page 11

Page 12

Page 13

Page 14

Page 15

Page 16

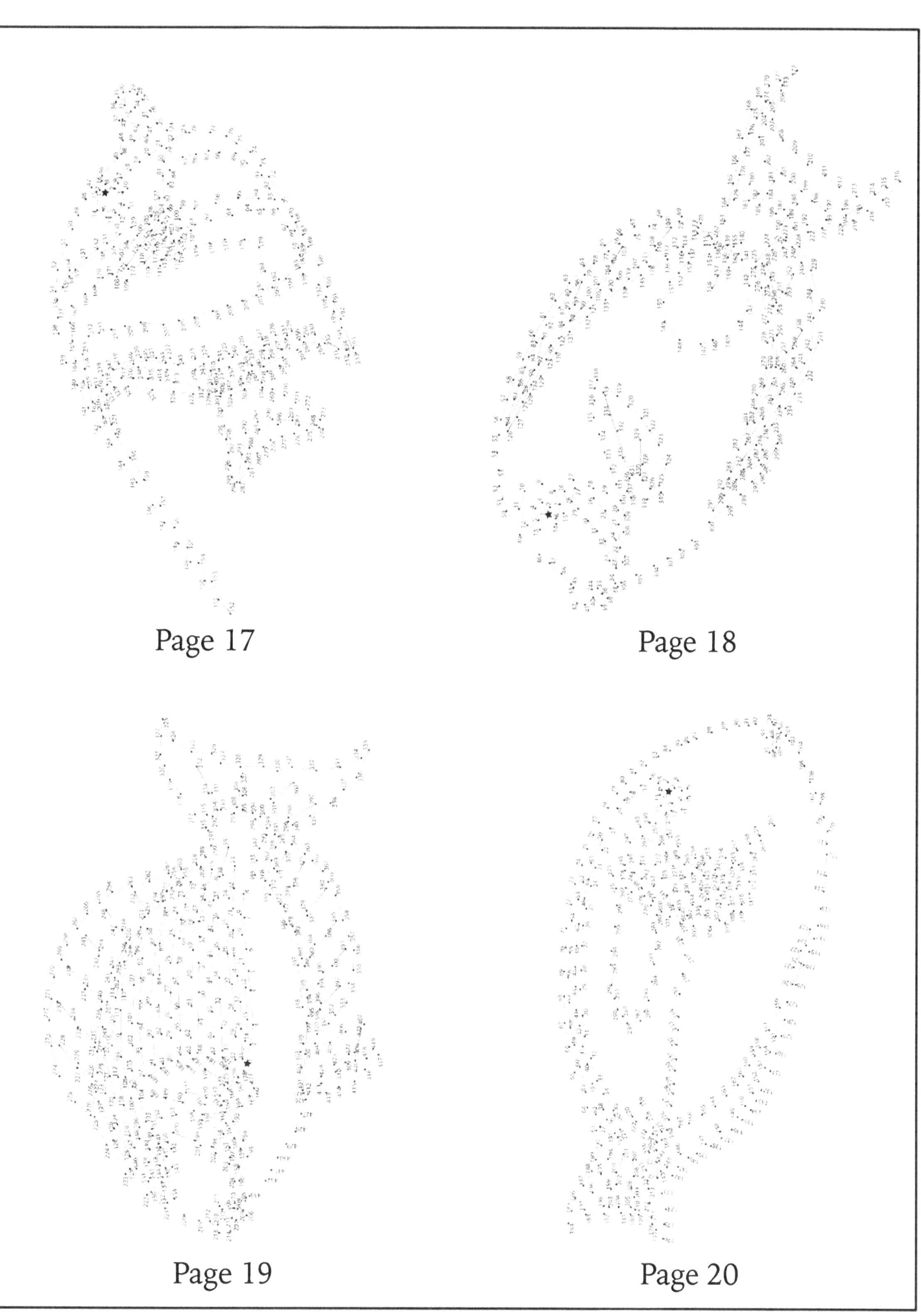

Page 17

Page 18

Page 19

Page 20